Rabbits and Hares

RABBITS
AND
HARES

Colleen Stanley Bare

Illustrated with photographs
by the author

DODD, MEAD & COMPANY • NEW YORK

ACKNOWLEDGMENT

The author wishes to thank Mark Bender, professional rabbit breeder and agriculture professor, for his technical assistance.

Text copyright © 1983 by Colleen Stanley Bare
Photographs copyright © 1983 by Colleen Stanley Bare
Printed in the United States of America

1 2 3 4 5 6 7 8 9 10

Library of Congress Cataloging in Publication Data

Bare, Colleen Stanley.
  Rabbits and hares.

  Includes index.
  Summary: Describes the characteristics and habits
of lagomorphs, generally, and of hares and various breeds
of rabbits.
  1. Rabbits—Juvenile literature. 2. Hares—Juvenile
literature. 3. Rabbit breeds—Juvenile literature.
[1. Rabbits. 2. Hares. 3. Rabbit breeds] I. Title.
QL737.L32B37   1983   599.32′2   82-45992
ISBN 0-396-08127-4

To Warren

Contents

Rabbits and Hares

Author's Note

I really enjoy taking pictures of the animals that I write about, because I can get to know them better by watching them and seeing what they do. Sometimes, however, wildlife can be very difficult to photograph, which was the case with the wild cottontails and hares. They presented three problems: I had trouble finding them; when I did find them, they immediately ran away; and there frequently wasn't enough daylight to get good photographs.

Wild rabbits and hares are afraid of humans; as soon as they see, hear, or smell one, they hide. They are also *crepuscular*, a scientific term meaning that they are usually only out in dim light, just after dawn and a little before dusk.

I dealt with these problems for many months, spending long hours watching, and waiting, for rabbits in fields, orchards, and vineyards. The best time, in the warm months, was about five o'clock in the morning, when the sun was an orangy ball hanging low over the fields, before the world had awakened to scare away the rabbits. Frequently I was disappointed. Often I couldn't get

11

close enough to photograph a single rabbit, while trudging between the rows in vineyards or as I sat very still in the cold dawn. But once in awhile, something exciting happened.

One day, I had been watching a cottontail through the long lens on my camera for quite awhile. The rabbit had also been watching me, with its big ears turned in my direction. I expected it to scurry into the bushes at any minute. Suddenly, it scratched at the ground, then moved a few feet, and plopped into an already prepared *form*. I couldn't believe what I was seeing. I had read all about rabbits' forms, which are where they rest during the day, but it was too good to be true to see this animal lying in one, sunning itself.

Another morning, as I walked through a field, a jackrabbit suddenly popped up and bounded right in front of me. My camera was ready, and I got the picture. My jackrabbit photography often required slow, careful stalking, sometimes for more than an hour— crawling on hands and knees, inching along until I could get close enough for a camera shot.

At times there were interruptions: farmers on tractors or in trucks, cows trailing me through fields, young hunters with blowguns stalking the same victims as I, my car getting stuck in the mud (twice), and dogs. My first encounter with a snarling dog was in a vineyard, when a large one raced toward me as I crouched behind a vine. He looked and sounded ferocious, and I was scared. When he got close, I began to speak softly to him, just as

Rabbits and hares are difficult to photograph.

12

I do to my own little city dog. "What a nice doggy, good doggy, sweet doggy, gentle doggy." At the very moment when it seemed as though he were going to eat me alive, he threw himself on his back, on top of my shoes, all four feet straight up in the air, and wagged his tail. Obviously, he was someone's pet, just doing his thing. After he had frightened away the rabbits and the photographers, he probably went back to the hearth. This technique worked on several other threatening canines, and two dogs at one farm became so friendly that they waited for me each morning out on the road and wouldn't leave me. Since rabbits and dogs don't mix, I finally had to seek other pastures.

The light problem persisted, solved only by using fast film, putting the camera on a tripod, slowing down the shutter speeds, and taking advantage of every little shaft of daylight.

Wild rabbits are built for escaping, and I learned that they do a marvelous job of it. By comparison, the tame rabbits are wonderful subjects; they almost smile for the camera.

1

The Wild and the Tame

One spring evening, before dusk, a baby male jackrabbit was nibbling on some tender dandelions in a grassy field, when he heard a sound. It was such a tiny sound that it was hardly a sound at all. But the jackrabbit heard, and he froze. He pressed his small body against the ground, buried his head in the grass, and stayed absolutely still. No part of him moved, not his whiskers nor his eyes or even his nose. With his speckled, brownish coloring, and his ears laid back, he could hardly be seen. From a distance, he looked more like a bush than a jackrabbit.

The noise that he had heard was the slight rustle of a leaf, stirring under the foot of a red fox. The fox was rabbit hunting, hoping to take dinner to his mate that lived in a nearby den with their newborn pups. The fox moved slowly and stealthily, his sharp eyes alert, and came within a few feet of the jackrabbit. But, seeing nothing, he soon moved on. The jackrabbit remained frozen for a long time, until he was sure that the fox was gone, and then darted away. Once again, he had been spared.

15

A baby jackrabbit hiding quietly in the grass

The life of the wild rabbit and of its near relative, the hare, is a series of close calls and escapes. Living in an unfriendly world, it is among the most preyed upon of all mammals, by many animal and bird predators and by human hunters. It must find food wherever it can, frequently from farmers' crops, which makes it an unwelcome guest. From birth, it is instinctively alert and always on guard, even while sleeping and eating. It is nervous and quick and secretive, because just about everyone and everything is trying to catch it.

How different is the life of the wild rabbit from that of its cousin, the tame rabbit. The tame rabbit lives with people. It is cared for, protected, and provided with food and suitable shelter.

16

When it is a pet, it often lives peacefully with some of the same animals that are the enemies of wild rabbits, like dogs and cats. It is usually gentle, meek, and easy to get along with. It doesn't have to be cautious and wary, because it is one of the country's most popular pets. Almost everyone likes the tame rabbit.

Foxes are predators of wild rabbits and hares.

2

History

Members of the rabbit family have been around for over 30 million years. Recent findings by geologists indicate that rabbits and opossums are the most ancient of known living mammals in America and Europe. Some say that rabbits came from Africa, and historians have found colored paintings of rabbits and hares in Spanish caves dating back twenty thousand years.

Man has made use of rabbits and hares throughout history. They were hunted for sport and for their meat by the ancient Egyptians and the Romans. Rabbits played an important role in the religious ceremonies of the Chinese around two thousand years ago. The primitive Aztecs and the American Indians also used rabbit meat for food and the skins for clothing. In the 1400s, the Portuguese sailors kept rabbits on their ships, to supply them with fresh meat during their long voyages. As recently as the 1800s, other sailing ships carried rabbits for the same reason.

People often meet rabbits for the first time in stories, such as the White Rabbit and the March Hare in *Alice's Adventures in*

18

Wonderland, or in cartoons like Bugs Bunny. Rabbits are in nursery rhymes:

> Bye, baby bunting,
> Daddy's gone a-hunting,
> To get a little rabbit's skin,
> To wrap a baby bunting in.

Many rabbit stories repeat a similar theme. The rabbit gets into trouble, is in danger of being killed, and escapes just in time. In Beatrix Potter's *The Tale of Peter Rabbit*, Peter disobeys his mother and raids Mr. McGregor's garden. He is almost caught by Mr. McGregor and barely gets away, to return to his mother and sisters, Flopsy, Mopsy, and Cotton-tail. Many of the Uncle Remus stories are about Br'er Rabbit who, even though he is weaker than his animal neighbors, is able to outsmart them through his cleverness. He particularly delights in tricking his old enemy, Br'er Fox, who is constantly trying to catch Br'er Rabbit. Although these are just fantasies, they truly reflect the dangers confronting the wild rabbit.

A more gentle fable is that told by Aesop, the Greek storyteller, called *The Hare and the Tortoise.* In the story a tortoise challenges a hare to a race. The speedy hare is so sure that he will win that, after the slow-moving tortoise has waddled away, the hare lies down and falls asleep. By the time he awakens, the tortoise is almost at the finish line, and the hare is too far behind to catch up. Aesop's moral from this tale is, "Slow but steady wins the race."

For centuries, rabbits and hares have been featured in some of the myths of the world. Early South American Indians thought that the hare created the universe. The Hindus believed that a hare lived on the moon and could be seen in the moon spots. The idea of the Easter bunny and Easter eggs comes from an old Teutonic legend in which the first rabbit was created from a bird by the spring goddess, Eostre. The rabbit was so grateful that it laid brightly colored eggs each year for a spring festival, named in her honor.

Even today, some people carry a rabbit's foot, supposedly to bring them good luck. One version of this superstition says that the left hind foot of a rabbit, carried into a churchyard at midnight under a full moon, will protect its owner from evil spirits.

Rabbits and hares are in our language. We use expressions like *scared as a rabbit* (easily frightened), *rabbit punch* (a sharp blow to the base of the neck), *harebrained* (reckless, foolish, unwise), *rabbit ears* (an indoor television antenna, with two telescoping aerials), *rabbit ball* (in baseball, a bouncy lively ball), *rabbit food* (slang expression for a green salad or raw vegetables), *jackrabbit start* (a quick start made by a car), *run like a jackrabbit* (very fast!).

Rabbits have often been featured in stories and tales.

Family Backgrounds

Rabbits and hares were once considered to be rodents. This was because of their continually growing, long front teeth that look like those of squirrels, gophers, mice, and other members of the order Rodentia. However, rabbits and hares have four upper front teeth instead of the rodents' two, have more cheek teeth, move their jaws differently when chewing, and have short tails. Because of such variations, scientists finally gave the rabbits and hares their own order, called Lagomorpha, a Greek word meaning "hare-shaped."

The lagomorphs are divided into two families. The principal one, Leporidae, consists of rabbits and hares. The smaller family, Ochotonidae, contains just the pika. The pika is a rare, hamster-sized rock rabbit.

The Leporidae family is made up of three genera: hares (*Lepus*), cottontails (*Sylvilagus*), and wild European rabbits and domestic rabbits (*Oryctolagus*). The wild European rabbits are ancestors of the tame rabbits that we raise in our country today.

*Jackrabbit skull. Lagomorphs have twenty-eight teeth
with six front incisors.*

There are a number of species of hares and rabbits throughout
the world, and of the cottontail in America. In fact, wild lagomorphs are almost everywhere, on all continents and in every
occupied land area, with the exception of Madagascar and Ant-
arctica. This is because they are so adaptable and can survive in
almost any habitat and climate, from sea level to high mountains,
and from hot deserts to the cold Arctic. They feed on vegetation
and usually live above ground, with the exception of the wild
European rabbit. This rabbit, often called the Old World rabbit,
is unusual because it digs burrows and lives in underground
colonies.

Some have said that the cottontail is "as American as apple
pie." It is our true native rabbit, existing only in North and South

America. The hare, which includes the American jackrabbit, is found in Europe, Africa, Asia, and North America. The wild European rabbit is in southern Europe, the British Isles, and North Africa, as well as in Australia and New Zealand where it was introduced in the 1800s. Some also still remain on remote, small islands scattered throughout the world and are the descendants of the wild European rabbits released from the early sailing ships. The little pika lives in the very high mountain regions of Asia, eastern Europe, British Columbia, and the northwestern United States.

Wild rabbits feed on vegetation.

Survival

Many lagomorphs are hares and not rabbits. Yet has anyone ever said to you, "I saw a hare today"? More likely, the person said, "I saw a rabbit today," or a "jackrabbit," or a "cottontail."

It is very confusing, because all jackrabbits are actually hares. The only *rabbits* that you are likely to find in the United States are the cottontails and the tame or domestic rabbits. So, how do rabbits and hares differ?

If you could see a hare and a cottontail together, side by side, you would notice that, although they resemble one another, they do not look exactly alike. For one thing, the hare is larger. Compared to the round little cottontail, the hare looks long and lanky. Hare ears are bigger, and the legs are longer and stronger than those of the cottontail. The two animals also move differently. The rabbit runs and scampers, while the hare hops and leaps. But the most important difference between rabbits and hares has to do with their young. Rabbit babies are born without fur, unable to see, hear, or walk, and are completely helpless. Newborn hares

Top: *Cottontails are runners.*
Bottom: *Jackrabbits are leapers.*

Top: *Cottontails and domestic rabbits are blind, hairless, and helpless at birth.* Bottom: *Baby jackrabbits have fur and can run and hop.*

Owls and eagles are predators of rabbits and hares.

come into the world fully furred, with their eyes open, and are able to hop almost immediately after birth.

Rabbits and hares do have much in common, especially their drive to stay alive. Their enemies' list is long and includes most meat-eating animals, such as foxes, coyotes, bobcats, badgers, wolves, weasels, martens, and skunks. House cats and domestic dogs raid rabbit nests and kill the young. Large birds—hawks, eagles, owls, and crows—swoop down and attack or capture both

28

babies and adults. But the greatest enemy is man. As popular game animals many rabbits are taken yearly by hunters—over two million cottontails in New York State and at least one million in California. California hunters also kill two million jackrabbits annually. At times, jackrabbits have become so abundant, and have done such crop damage in the Midwest, that ranchers have organized jackrabbit hunts, sometimes killing thousands in a single drive. Idaho farmers killed over 100,000 during several hunts in 1982. Many rabbits and hares are accidentally destroyed by farm machinery and automobiles. And, the young often die by drowning, or from becoming chilled, during stormy weather.

By now, you may wonder how the lagomorph clan, faced with such adversity, survives at all.

Farmers put milk cartons around young trees to protect them from hungry jackrabbits.

DEFENSES

Country dogs delight in chasing cottontails and jackrabbits through fields and orchards. Yet farmers report that unless their dogs are trained hunters, they rarely can catch a rabbit. And, if they do, it is likely to be a very young, old, or sick one. This is because nature has provided rabbits and hares with special survival equipment.

For one thing, they have oversized ears, with uncanny hearing ability. Each ear is able to swivel independently, in different directions, picking up even the slightest sounds of danger, sometimes from hundreds of feet away. By the time a dog has spotted a jackrabbit and taken a few steps, the "jack" has heard and is

This cottontail has one ear turned forward, the other backward, to detect sounds from both directions.

Note the blood vessels in the ears of this captive jackrabbit

Jackrabbit eyes are large and protruding.

bounding away. These unusual ears also help to regulate the animal's body temperature. Each ear contains many blood vessels through which blood is pumped, to give off heat during hot weather. In cold weather, the blood flowing through the ears is reduced, and heat is conserved.

Lagomorph eyes are also special. Large and protruding, they are set high on each side of the head. This provides an almost complete circle of vision, so that the rabbit or hare can catch sight of an enemy coming from most directions. And when the animal can't see or hear its predator, it usually can smell him with its sensitive, twitching nose.

The eating habits of wild rabbits and hares help them to survive. Although they prefer grasses and green vegetation, they eat

Close-up of jackrabbit eye

about anything that grows and can find food almost anywhere. They can live on plants, shrubs, cactus in dry areas, most crops such as fruits, vegetables, alfalfa, and grains, as well as a winter diet of twigs, shoots, roots, dried grasses, and the bark of many trees. They do not require water, except during periods of drought and very hot weather. Ordinarily, they get enough moisture from vegetation and from licking the dewdrops on plants.

33

All lagomorphs, wild and tame, digest much of their food twice, by eating a portion of their droppings. This process is called *coprophagy*. The undigested food passes out of the body, through the anus, in the form of moist, soft pellets. Immediately, the rabbit or hare eats these pellets, which are rich in B vitamins and give the animal important added nutrition. This usually occurs at night, and the soft pellets are different from the hard, dry ones dropped during the daytime, which are not eaten. Rabbit breeders claim that if a rabbit is unable to practice coprophagy, it will suffer from a serious vitamin deficiency and may die.

Rabbits and hares are able to remain motionless for long periods of time. Since their coat color is usually the same as their habitat, by "freezing" they become practically invisible to predators. When a jackrabbit sees a dog, it will crouch down low in the brush, with its ears laid back, and remain frozen until the dog leaves. However, if the jack is forced into a chase, it can often elude the swiftest of its enemies by running in a zigzag pattern, dodging, twisting, and turning.

If a dog should be fortunate enough to capture a cottontail or a jackrabbit, he may still be the loser. The animal will vigorously fight for its life, biting, scratching with sharp claws, and kicking with its powerful hind legs and large feet. It will give a loud, piercing scream when caught, sometimes causing the startled dog, or other attacker, to drop it—allowing the rabbit to escape. Although rabbits and hares are mostly silent, they may thump their feet at the sound of danger, often as a warning signal to others.

But if they can't outwit or outrun their enemies, at least, as a species, they can outbreed them. Lagomorphs are able to produce exceptionally large numbers of young each year. This is important, because 85 percent of all cottontails and 70 percent of all hares die before their first birthdays, with an average life-span of one year for any one individual animal. However, without this high mortality, the country would be overrun with cottontails and hares. For example, if a pair of cottontails were to produce four litters of five rabbits per litter each year, and if all of these rabbits survived, by the end of five years there would be over 300,000 rabbits descended from just this one original pair. Something like this actually happened in Australia.

Originally, there were no rabbits in Australia. In 1859, an English settler imported a dozen pair of wild European rabbits from Great Britain, to use them as game animals. He placed them on an estate in the Australian province of Victoria, and they soon

Nervous jackrabbit, frozen—listening, looking, sniffing

Top: *Rabbits groom themselves. They lick their paws . . .*
Bottom: *. . . and wash their faces.*

escaped. The rabbits multiplied, and in just a few years there were millions, because there were no natural predators in Australia to control them. Thousands of acres of grass and sheep grazing lands were eaten by the hungry rabbits. Frantic measures were taken to try to destroy them, using guns, poison, traps, and the building of a 2,000-mile rabbit fence. But nothing worked, and the rabbits kept increasing. Finally, some sick rabbits, infected with a deadly rabbit disease called myxomatosis were deliberately released into the countryside. The disease spread quickly, through direct contact and by mosquitoes carrying the virus from sick rabbits to healthy ones. The result was the death of millions of rabbits. The land soon became green again, and the farmers could raise their sheep and crops.

Myxomatosis is only fatal to the wild European rabbit and does not affect cottontails or hares. However, all wild lagomorphs are susceptible to a serious disease called tularemia, or rabbit fever, which can be transmitted to humans. They also get tapeworms.

All lagomorphs carefully groom themselves, washing their fur much like a cat. They even clean all four feet and in between the toes, pull down each ear with the front feet for a thorough licking, and wash their tails. Despite such cleanliness, wild rabbits and hares become infested with parasites such as ticks, mites, fleas, and lice. Mosquitoes and flies become very bothersome in the summertime.

There are a number of species of cottontail rabbits and hares, and two of the pikas, living in North America.

5

Cottontail Rabbits

The cottontail is our all-American rabbit. It is probably the best-known wild animal in the country, because it exists in almost every state and locality. There are thirteen species in all of North and South America, with six major ones in the United States. These are: the eastern cottontail (*Sylvilagus floridanus*), occurring in most of the states east of the Rocky Mountains and into Arizona; the Audubon or desert variety (*Sylvilagus auduboni*), found in most of the southwestern half of the country; the mountain rabbit, also called Nuttall's cottontail, (*Sylvilagus nuttalli*), in North Dakota and all of the western states; the marsh rabbit (*Sylvilagus palustris*), living in the coastal states from Virginia down to Florida and Alabama; the swamp rabbit (*Sylvilagus aquaticus*), in the Gulf States, except Florida, extending north as far as southern Illinois; and the brush rabbit (*Sylvilagus bachmani*), of the Far West.

All these cottontails are similar in appearance and habits. They are easily recognized by the cottontail emblem—a white, powder-puff tail that resembles a cotton ball and actually helps the animal to survive. During a chase, it is this flashing, bouncing "white flag" that the hunter or other predator sees in the distance. Suddenly, the rabbit stops and sits, hidden in the bushes, leaving the pursuer trying to figure out what happened to the "flag." Scientists call this the "flash pattern" escape of the cottontail.

Everyone thinks of the cottontail as being very shy and timid, and most of the time it really is. It is often smaller and weaker than its enemies, averaging 15 inches in length, and 2 to 4 pounds in weight, with 2- to 3-inch ears. But, there are occasional stories of true cottontail courage, where the rabbit has fought off large

A young brush rabbit

The cottontail emblem is a white, powder-puff tail.

dogs, foxes, skunks, snakes, crows, and even its bitter foe, the weasel. Mother cottontails will defend their nests with ferocity, and may attack humans who get too close. In a scientific experiment, a cottontail was placed in a cage with an adult male bobcat, several times its size. When the bobcat moved in for the kill, the plucky rabbit whacked him several times in the face, using a hind foot. This so surprised the bobcat that he retreated to a corner, where he sat staring for hours.

Cottontails usually live where there is thick underbrush, along the borders of fields and woods, close to their diet of green vegetation. Unlike many other small mammals, they do not dig burrows. They make shallow depressions in the ground called *forms*,

Cottontail country—thick underbrush with lots of cover

where they rest during the day, coming out at twilight to feed from dusk until early morning. A rabbit may have several forms, one for sunning, another under a bush for keeping cool, always located so that it can watch for enemies. When it is very hot and dry, or extremely cold and windy, cottontails may move into the abandoned holes of burrowing animals such as badgers, woodchucks, and ground squirrels. They are rarely adventuresome and

Cottontail starting to scratch out a form.

Cottontail lies in its form, sunning on a cool morning.

usually spend their lives in a small area, perhaps no bigger than a large city block.

The cottontail molts twice a year, its coat becoming thinner and lighter in summer and heavier for the cold of winter. Its colors, varying from peppered brown to tan or grayish, blend well with the surroundings of trees and bushes and give the animal a protective camouflage. However, if a cottontail is caught out in the open, it can speed along at eighteen to twenty miles an hour, bounding up to fifteen feet, until it can dive into some brushy cover or a borrowed hole.

Cottontails use abandoned ground squirrel burrows.

The female cottontail first mates at about six months and, twenty-eight days later, produces an average of five babies. She usually has four or five such litters a year, with the breeding season lasting from February until September. During this time, the male rabbits have spirited battles that sometimes prove fatal to the loser. The winner then courts the female, with much leaping through the air to show his bravery and strength. Following the mating, the female drives him away.

A few days before giving birth, the female digs a bowl-shaped nest, about four inches deep and six inches across, in a sheltered spot such as under a bush or in a clump of tall grass. She lines the nest with dried grasses and with fur that she has pulled from her chest. If the babies are born out in the open, which sometimes happens, she carries them, one at a time, back to the prepared nest. There, she nurses them and then covers the nest with a blanket that she has made of grasses and her fur. This covering both hides the babies and helps keep them warm. The mother often mates again that same day.

The female cottontail is a good mother. She stays in a form nearby, watching the nest, ready to fight any intruder that might find the hidden babies. She doesn't return to them until dark, when she carefully removes the blanket and nurses them, usually three or four times during the night.

Cottontails are able to hide their young remarkably well. Their nests are sometimes located in very unlikely places, such as in dense, thorny bramblebushes, or hidden in brush bordering golf courses. Litters have even been raised in small trees, where the mother has been able to climb up to nine feet and build a nest in a tangle of covering branches.

The babies grow rapidly. At the end of the first week, they have fur, can see and hear, and soon venture out of the nest for short periods. They begin to sample grasses and plants, and, at age three weeks, no longer need their mother's milk. By the time the mother is ready to give birth to a new family, they are completely on their own. They now scatter into a dangerous world.

6

Hares and Pikas

There are four main species of the North American hare: the black-tailed jackrabbit (*Lepus californicus*), the white-tailed jackrabbit (*Lepus townsendi*), the snowshoe or varying hare (*Lepus americanus*), and the Arctic hare (*Lepus arcticus*). These differ in their habitat and in the color of their winter coats. But they are alike in their habits and in their powerful instinct to escape. If they are lucky enough to survive infancy, they soon know every foot of their ten acres of territory. Wherever they may live, each path, roadway, shrub, rock, gully, or grassy area becomes a familiar escape route or a place to hide.

The black-tailed jackrabbit roams the plains and open grasslands of much of the western half of the United States, and has even been transplanted to New England's Nantucket Island and Martha's Vineyard. Being very adaptable, it sometimes lives in fields near cities and becomes a hazard for the airplanes around

Jackrabbit country—open grasslands

The black-tailed jackrabbit is really a hare.

airports. It was originally called "jackass rabbit" by the pioneer settlers of the Southwest, because of its huge 7-inch, black-tipped ears. Later shortened to jackrabbit, the animal is really a jackhare. It is of average hare size (21 inches long, weight 6 pounds), and average hare color (grayish brown), and is smaller than another black-tailed variety, the 8-pound antelope jackrabbit (*Lepus*

48

alleni) of Arizona. The black-tailed jackrabbit's tail color immediately identifies it from the white-tailed jackrabbit.

The white-tailed jackrabbit is slightly larger than the black-tailed and lives farther north. In its northernmost ranges, where there is winter snow, its fur changes color twice a year during the molting process. Its brown-gray summer coat is gradually replaced by a thick white one for winter. This color change is brought about by increasing, or decreasing, daylight. The amount of light passing through the animal's eyes affects its pituitary gland, which controls the amount of color pigment going into the coat. The change is very important to the hare's survival, to camouflage it. A predator has difficulty seeing a white animal in white snow.

The snowshoe hare, named for its large, furry hind feet, lives

Left: *Snowshoe hare in its winter coat.* Right: *Snowshoe hare in its summer coat. (Photographed at The Oakland Museum.)*

in the mountain ranges of eastern and western United States. It is also called the varying hare, because of its changing color—brown in summer and white in winter. It is the smallest of the hares, at 3 pounds and 18 inches long. In its snowy habitat, the snowshoe hare has an additional important enemy—the lynx.

The largest of the hare family is the Arctic hare, measuring up to 27 inches and averaging 12 pounds. This is the hare of the frozen north in Alaska, Greenland, and northern Canada. Its coat remains white all year round except in its southern range, where it is brownish gray in summer. Two of its predators, the Arctic fox and the weasel, also have white winter coats.

Breeding season for hares is in the spring and summer, though it can be longer in warmer climates. Mating behavior is similar to the cottontails', with rival males battling for dominance. Females begin breeding at age one year, with an average of four babies born thirty-six days (snowshoe) to forty-two days (jackrabbits and Arctic hare) after mating. The babies, sometimes called *leverets*, weigh 2 to 4 ounces at birth. Hares usually produce two to three litters a year. Unlike the cottontail, the hare mother does not prepare a nest. When the babies are born, she nurses them and hides them individually in different locations. She returns to each hideaway at night, to feed her young. The babies, already furred and hopping at birth, become independent very quickly.

The hare, like the cottontail, spends its days resting and watching. It huddles in a form that it has scraped out in a protected spot, often under a bush. With its long legs folded under its body,

50

Jackrabbit ready to run.

and the ears flattened against its back, it can hardly be seen. If danger threatens, the hare freezes, always ready to burst into action and leap from a sitting position into a dead run if necessary. The hare remains in its form until twilight, when it emerges to feed on vegetation through the night. At dawn, it stops eating and often takes a dust bath, rolling in the dirt to free itself of parasites before returning to its form. It has usually eaten steadily

51

Jackrabbits are the broad jumpers of the lagomorphs.

through the night, consuming about three-quarters of a pound of food. Hares have big appetites, and twelve jackrabbits can eat as much as one sheep.

Snowshoe hares have been clocked at thirty miles per hour and are able to cover fifteen feet in one leap. However, the jackrabbits are the true broad jumpers of the lagomorph clan, leaping twenty-two feet in a single jump. The jacks are masters of escape, and their enemies have trouble catching them as they zigzag across their territories at speeds up to forty miles an hour.

PIKAS

The pika is a lagomorph of the high mountains, from 8,000 feet to more than 14,000 feet. There are two similar species: *Ochotona princeps* in western North America, from central California and north New Mexico to middle British Columbia, and *Ochotona collaris* (sometimes considered a subspecies) of Alaska and northern Canada. It is tiny, 6 to 8 inches long and weighing 5 ounces. It looks like a guinea pig rather than a rabbit, with small, rounded ears, short legs, and no visible tail.

Pikas live in colonies in rocky areas and spend most of their summer daytime hours gathering plants and grasses for future use. They spread these out on rocks to dry in the sun, adding to them daily. They then store these haypiles beneath overhanging boulders, or in rocky crevices, and this becomes their food supply during the cold winter months.

Pikas have the lagomorph tooth structure (twenty-eight teeth with the typical six front incisors), and they practice coprophagy.

53

Unlike rabbits and hares, they are very vocal and give repeated whistling calls to each other.

The female pika usually has one or two litters of two to four babies, born from May to July. The young are born approximately thirty days after mating and are lightly furred, blind, and helpless. By the end of the first week, they can see, walk, and bark, and are fully grown at six weeks. Now they must make their own haystacks and find a rocky home for the long winter ahead.

Pika predators include weasels, martens, hawks, and owls.

Pikas live among the rocks in the high mountains.

54

7

Cottontail and Jackrabbit Watching

Cottontails and jackrabbits are everywhere, except in cities and where there are many people. When you are in the country, sometimes not very far from towns, you can often see rabbits running through fields and orchards. If you look carefully, you may spot a pair of ears sticking up in some tall grass, and the glint of a dark eye staring at you—a cottontail for sure. Or a hare-shaped figure may be sitting at the edge of an orchard path, its huge ears swiveled in your direction—an alert jackrabbit. When you are walking through a field and come upon a jack in its form, it may practically explode in front of you, leaping four feet from a resting position, up and away.

In cottontail country, you can sometimes hear the rabbits eating, munching, and crunching in some heavy brush, even though you can't see them. If you sit on the ground nearby and wait, one may come out. But as soon as it spots you, it will freeze—and, if you're too close, it will scurry silently back into the brush.

55

*A hare-shaped figure may be sitting
at the edge of an orchard path.*

Twilight, just before dusk or just at dawn, is the best time for rabbit watching. It helps to wear earth-colored clothing, browns and greens, to make you less noticeable. A pair of binoculars is also useful. National and state wildlife refuges are good places to find rabbits, because the wildlife there is protected from hunters. But you must be patient, stay still, and wait.

If you should find a young cottontail or a baby jackrabbit, it is best not to pick it up. Rabbits and hares can quickly go into shock when they are handled by humans and sometimes literally die of fright. Wild rabbits are very difficult to raise. They either may die from improper feeding, or they escape—which they are determined to do.

56

Sometimes farmers try to raise orphaned newborn jackrabbits or cottontails. One farm family was successful in keeping a baby jackrabbit in their home for several months. The tiny male hare, just the size of the palm of a hand, was found in a field. He grew rapidly on a diet of milk, rolled oats, and raw vegetables, and lived in a box in the corner of the kitchen. Soon he hopped around the

A rabbit may be munching away at vegetation.

This captive jackrabbit is very nervous and ready to run.

house, jumping onto the backs of furniture, and scratched on the refrigerator door when he was hungry. Finally, when he was several months old and had become large, he began to bare his teeth at the family members. When he started to scratch and bite them, they released him back into the field.

58

Watchful, even while drinking milk

Other owners have reported that even when they have success-
fully nurtured wild rabbits through infancy, the animals rarely
lose their wildness. They remain scared, wide-eyed, and wary,
and never become completely domesticated.

So if you want to have a pet rabbit, you should get a tame one.

8

Domestic Rabbits

A lean-bodied, long-eared jackrabbit races at top speed through the tall grass of an open field, pursued by a coyote. Always wary and excitable, the hare leads the existence of the hunted and is running for its life.

At the same time, its close relative, a round-bodied, short-eared Netherland Dwarf tame rabbit sits quietly in a cage, contentedly chewing on some hay. It awaits the arrival of a human being, bringing food pellets and fresh water. The rabbit is relaxed, calm, and trusting.

How different are these two! Yet both are lagomorphs.

Tame rabbits, often called domestic rabbits, have the same lagomorph characteristics as their wild counterparts. This includes the typical tooth structure, wide vision, hypersensitive ears that help to regulate their temperatures, and the function of coprophagy. But they have very distinct life-styles, for one important rea-

Jackrabbits can run at forty miles an hour.

Netherland Dwarf—a trusting, tame rabbit

son. Cottontails and hares are wild animals, whereas tame rabbits are really domesticated farm animals.

Not that rabbits can only be raised on farms—far from it! A small rabbit can get along fine in a cage just 24″ x 24″ x 18″, and millions live in their owners' houses, garages, or backyards.

All domestic rabbits, regardless of breed, size, or color, are the descendents of the wild European rabbit. They belong to the same species, *Oryctolagus cuniculus*. Many people think that domestic rabbits can breed with cottontails and hares, but this is not true. Cottontails and hares are of different species (within the genera *Sylvilagus* and *Lepus*) and, generally, animals are not able to breed with those of another species.

Records indicate that rabbits probably first were domesticated in France in the sixteenth century. Monks, living in monasteries, kept rabbits in protected enclosures and bred them selectively. This same kind of selective breeding is used today, to improve existing rabbit breeds and develop new ones—by mating together rabbits with desired traits, so as to pass these on to their young. These desirable characteristics often have to do with size, fur quality, color, markings, and temperament.

Rabbit raising did not become widespread in the United States until the late 1800s, when a rabbit called the Belgian Hare was introduced into this country. Its hare-shaped body and long, hare-like ears probably account for its name, although it is really a tame rabbit and not a hare at all. Originally from Flanders in Belgium, it became a popular show rabbit in England before making its first appearance in the New England states. By 1900 a "Belgian Hare boom" had occurred in America, and some outstanding animals were sold for $300 apiece, which was a great deal of money at that time. It wasn't long before other rabbit breeds were imported from Europe and, from these, several new races were developed in the United States, including New Zealands, Californians, and Palominos. Gradually, more breeds were produced until, today, there are more than forty.

Rabbit business

Rabbits have become "big business" in the United States. With more than 12 million raised each year, they are used not only as pets and show animals, but for research, food, and fur. Over a million rabbits annually play important roles in research and

The Belgian Hare—first domestic rabbit in the United States

laboratory testing, at places like cancer research centers, university hospitals, and U.S. Public Health and pharmaceutical laboratories. Rabbits react to disease and medicines much like humans, so they have been used to develop tests and drugs for diseases like diabetes, diphtheria, tuberculosis, cancer, and heart disease. The effects of food additives, special diets, and skin creams have also been tested on rabbits. The New Zealand White is the breed most commonly chosen for laboratory purposes.

The New Zealand White is also the number one meat rabbit in the country. This industry is growing steadily, with many millions of pounds of rabbit meat produced every year. The largest processing operations are in the Ozarks and Southern California, although a number of small backyard breeders are in the business. The meat of domestic rabbits is all white, high in protein

New Zealand Whites are often used in scientific research.

and low in cholesterol, and fanciers say that it can be prepared in three hundred different ways.

Have you ever worn a felt hat? If so, the hat was probably made of rabbit fur. This fur is also used in the manufacture of upholstery and clothing, particularly coats, capes, muffs, and mittens. Some rabbit breeds have been especially developed for their fur. Examples are the Rex rabbit, with an unusually short, thick lustrous coat, and the Satin rabbit, famous for its dense, velvety fur. The Angora rabbit has long, silky hair that is called wool rather than fur, and is often spun into a fine, soft yarn for blankets, sweaters, socks, and other warm garments.

Rabbits have other more unusual uses, such as their nitrogen-rich manure being utilized as a high-grade fertilizer. Recently, domestic rabbits have helped out in the conservation of energy. A large number were placed in a nursery hothouse, where extra warmth was required for growing plants. The rabbits produced so much body heat that the high temperature of the room could be maintained without wasting precious fuel. The problem with this, of course, is that the rabbits had to receive plenty of their own kind of fuel—food!

Rabbit raising

Most owners will be glad to tell you that domestic rabbits make perfect pets, especially their own particular breeds. Not only are rabbits gentle and affectionate, they are also clean and easy to take care of. They can be housebroken just like a cat, using a litter box, and can be trained to do a few tricks such as jumping

Rabbits are clean pets. A Belgian Hare washing its face.

through a hoop. They don't require much space and can be kept outdoors, if their cages, or hutches, are well protected from extremes of weather. Rabbits don't howl at the moon, crow at dawn, or have loud meowing fights in the middle of the night. The noises they do make are soft, purring sounds of contentment, an occasional excited grunt or growl, and the small squeals of the young. Rabbits only speak loudly when they are injured or very frightened.

Rabbits have simple needs, but they do require daily care. They must have proper food, water, clean and adequately sized cages, and extra attention if you intend to breed them. Although they are basically healthy, if their hutches are not kept dry and sanitary, they can get diseases like colds, pneumonia, sore feet or hocks, ear canker, mites, and worms. Other ailments to worry about are heat exhaustion in the summertime, a liver disease called coccidiosis, and, in areas where there are mosquitoes, myxomatosis. An effective vaccine has been developed to prevent this disease in domestic rabbits.

Times have changed in rabbit raising. The old-fashioned wooden hutches, often built out of packing boxes or orange crates, are no longer considered desirable—nor is a diet of carrots, cabbage, and lettuce. Nowadays you can buy or build well-designed, sturdy wire cages that are easily cleaned and long lasting. Inexpensive gadgets for automatic feeding and watering make rabbit raising even easier.

The best rabbit food does not come from the garden. Livestock nutritionists have spent many years developing special, bite-sized food pellets for rabbits, providing the animals with everything they need for a well-balanced, healthful diet. These come in economical sacks and can be purchased at pet and farm supply stores.

Domestic rabbits are more like wild cottontails than jackrabbits in the birth and care of their young. The babies are born about thirty to thirty-one days after mating and, like the cottontails, are hairless, blind, deaf, and totally helpless. Unlike the wild rabbits, however, the domestic mother cannot prepare a nest in the ground under a bush, so several days before the expected birth, a "nest box" must be placed in her cage. This is an open-ended, small wire or wooden box, filled with straw. Here the mother builds a nest, using fur pulled from her own body for the lining. She also uses her hair to cover the newborns in cold weather, much like the wild cottontail's covering of her young with a blanket

Mini lop babies in their nest box

Left: *Rabbits should be picked up by the back of the neck, while supporting the hindquarters.* Right: *Because of his great size, this Flemish Giant gets carried backwards.*

made from grasses and fur. The babies do not open their eyes for ten days, and they are weaned at six to eight weeks. Female domestic rabbits, referred to as *does*, usually produce an average of eight babies in a litter, and can safely have four or five litters per year. The males are called *bucks*.

Rabbit breeds

It isn't easy to select a rabbit breed, when there are more than forty to choose from. Many of these come in a variety of colors, which makes the decision even more difficult. Some say that any

70

breed of rabbit will make a good pet, if you start giving it affection when it is very young and take excellent care of it. Pet rabbits like to be held and fondled, but you should never pick up one by its sensitive ears or by its legs. The correct way to lift a rabbit is by the loose skin at the back of its neck, while supporting its hindquarters with the other hand. A good method of carrying it is under the arm.

The American Rabbit Breeders Association sets certain *standards*, which are a list of specific physical requirements representing perfection, for each breed. The word *breed* refers to a group of animals, in this case rabbits, which, when mated together, will reproduce offspring that always have the same characteristics in size, shape, fur texture, markings, and growth. Domestic rabbits are usually purebreds. This means that all of their relatives, including parents, grandparents, and great-grandparents, are alike and of the same breed. Many rabbit breeds are divided into *varieties*, referring to different fur colors. Some have definite *markings*, which means that the basic coat color (usually white) is broken up by fur of a different color, arranged in a definite, specified pattern. Examples of this are the Dutch and Tan rabbits.

Most domestic rabbit breeds not only do not resemble wild rabbits and hares, many of them do not even look like each other. They may differ in size, shape, length, coloring, and in fur texture. The largest ones are called *giants*, weighing up to 15 or more pounds, and the smallest weigh 2 to 3 pounds. Most have short coats, except for the Angora rabbit whose long, thick wool can be sheared off and sold.

The oldest rabbit breeds were originally imported from Europe. Most of the newer breeds developed in this country are the result of careful selective breeding, to produce rabbits for special purposes such as for fur, meat, show, or as pets. An example of this is the Californian rabbit, which was selectively bred from a combination of the Chinchilla, Himalayan, and New Zealand White rabbits. The New Zealand White is the result of combining several breeds, including the Flemish Giant, the American White, and the Angora. It is interesting to learn how different breeds originated.

Below are some representative breeds.

Angora. The Angora requires more grooming than any other rabbit because of its beautiful, soft 3-inch-long coat. It can give 4 ounces of wool every three months but, even when it is a pet, its coat must be clipped at least once a year. First recorded in France in 1723, it was imported into the United States from England in 1920. There are two kinds, the English Angora weighing 5½ to 6½ pounds, and the French Angora at 8 or more pounds. They come in white, black, and several colors.

Belgian Hare. Called the "race horse of the rabbit family," the Belgian Hare's long, lean, arched body and slender legs make it an interesting show rabbit. The first domestic rabbit in America, it is a deep reddish-tan color and weighs 7 to 9 pounds. Breeders claim that it is very alert, intelligent, and exceptionally active, requiring an extra large hutch—especially for jumping!

Californian. Developed in America, first shown in California in 1928, the Californian is an important show and meat animal.

Top: *Angora, white.* Bottom: *Belgian Hare.*

Top: *Californians*. Bottom: *Champagne D'Argent*.

American Checkered Giant

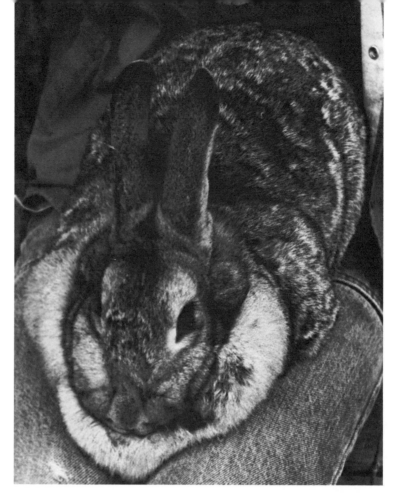

Top: *Chinchilla*. Bottom: *Dutch*.

It is medium-large, 8 to 10½ pounds, and is all white with a black nose, ears, feet, and tail.

Champagne D'Argent. Baby Champagne D'Argents are unusual because they are born with black coats that gradually become silver by age four months. One of the oldest breeds, mentioned in a French journal in 1730, it originally came from a French province called Champagne. Hence, its name means "silver rabbit from Champagne." Weight is from 9 to 12 pounds.

American Checkered Giant. This large rabbit, weighing 11 to 12 pounds, was probably developed mainly from the Flemish Giant in Belgium, although it was imported into this country from Germany in 1910. It has unique black or blue markings circling its eyes, on the nose, cheeks, ears and tail, down its spine, and on its sides.

Chinchilla. There are three Chinchilla rabbit breeds: standard (5½ to 8 pounds), American (9 to 12 pounds), and giant (12 to 15 pounds). They are in no way related to the chinchilla mammal, a South American rodent. However, their coats resemble the chinchilla rodent's in color, a rich blue-gray, making the rabbits valuable as show and fur animals. The breed was first shown in France in 1913, received the "prize of honor" at the Paris Exposition of 1914, and a silver cup valued at $1,000 was offered for the best Chinchilla rabbit in England in 1917. It also became an instant sensation in the United States rabbit world when it arrived here two years later.

Dutch. Handsome and very popular as a pet, the Dutch is a small rabbit (3½ to 5½ pounds) with a short, compact body and a two-tone coat. With white on its face and circling its body, it also has a number of typical Dutch markings in a variety of colors, including chocolate, black, blue, gray, and tortoise (orange). It originated in Holland and was in England by 1864, making it another of the older breeds.

English Spot. Because of its very exact markings, which are difficult to achieve, it is said that some English rabbit breeders have spent lifetimes trying to produce the "ideal" English Spot. Another of the oldest show breeds, exhibited in England since 1884, it weighs 5 to 8 pounds. It comes in several varieties (black, blue, chocolate, gold, gray, lilac, tortoise), has a distinctive butterfly mark on its nose, and is considered to be an excellent pet.

Flemish Giant. The largest of all of the domestic breeds, weighing up to 15 pounds, the Flemish Giant needs an oversized hutch and a large amount of food. Originating in Flanders, Belgium, its varieties include black, blue, light gray, fawn, sandy, steel gray, and white. It is a true giant, with a massive body and heavy limbs, and receives a lot of attention and admiration at rabbit shows.

Blanc de Hotot. This 9- to 11-pound breed was named after the French region of Hotot-en-Ange, where it was originally developed. Its outstanding characteristic is its eye markings—thin, deep, black bands circling each eye. The coat is snowy white over the entire body, except for the eye bands.

Harlequin. The Harlequin is another "show stopper." It attracts great interest because of its spectacular markings, arranged in colorful bands around its body. Weighing 6 to 9 pounds, the Harlequins come in two groups, Japanese and Magpie, with

Top: *English Spot.* Bottom: *This prize-winning Flemish Giant is large and lovable. He has been a winner at shows and is a Grand Champion.*

Blanc de Hotot

Top: *Harlequin*. Bottom: *Mini Lop—Broken variety*.

several varieties—black, blue, chocolate, and lilac. In the Japanese, the colors alternate with orange. In the Magpie, they alternate with white. The rabbit is of French origin and was first shown in Paris in 1887.

Lops. Long ears that droop, or hang down, are the outstanding feature of the Lops. One of the oldest breeds, appearing in England by 1810, there are several kinds of Lops. These include the English Lop, with ear lengths of 25 inches or more and weighing 9 to 11 pounds, the French Lop at 9 to 12 pounds, the Mini Lop at 4½ to 6½ pounds, and the small 3-pound Holland Lop. All Lops come in solid or mixed colorings, and owners sometimes call them the "lovable Lops."

Netherland Dwarf. The smallest of all the breeds, about the size of a large guinea pig, this little rabbit is from the Netherlands. Weighing 2 to 2½ pounds, with tiny 2-inch long ears, it comes in a wide variety of colors and color combinations. A popular pet, its miniature size makes it particularly desirable where space is at a premium.

New Zealand. The name has nothing to do with its origin, for the New Zealand is an all-American rabbit and the country's current favorite. It is medium-large, 9 to 12 pounds, and comes in white, black, and red. The red variety was developed first, in the early 1900s, followed by the New Zealand White in the 1920s and the Black in the 1950s. New Zealand Whites are often sold in pet shops and are the typical white bunnies purchased as pets at Eastertime.

Top: *French Lop.* Bottom: *Owner with young Netherland Dwarf.*

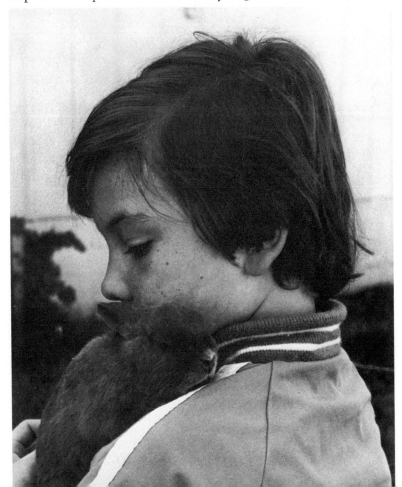

Top: *New Zealand—Black variety*. Bottom: *Rex—Chinchilla variety*.

Top: *Rex—Broken variety*. Bottom: *Rhinelander*.

Rex. This important fur rabbit was developed in France about 1919. Its short coat comes in many colors, including black, blue, castor (chestnut brown), chinchilla, lilac, red, sable, and seal white. It is midweight, 7½ to 10½ pounds, and its pelt is prized for fur coats.

Rhinelander. Another unique rabbit and a favorite at shows, the Rhinelander has distinctive black and bright orange markings. Of medium size, 6½ to 10 pounds, it has a colored stripe running from the nape of the neck to the end of the tail, a butterfly mark on the nose, and eye circles.

Satin. An American breed, appearing in 1931, the Satin is noted for its shiny, satinlike coat. Its dense fur, about an inch long, comes in deep rich colors, including red, chocolate, black, blue, copper, and one called Siamese, resembling the color of a Siamese cat. It weighs from 8½ to 11 pounds and is greatly admired at shows.

Silver-Marten. Known in England as the Silver Fox rabbit, and originally developed from the Chinchilla, this breed has a silver circle around each eye. It weighs 6½ to 9½ pounds and is in varieties of black, blue, chocolate, and sable.

Tan. The special feature of the Tan is a uniform "tan pattern," in the form of a triangle, running from behind the ears to the center of the shoulders. Produced in England in the 1880s, the first Tans were only in black. Now, they are also bred in blue, chocolate, and lilac, each with the tan markings. These are small rabbits, weighing 4 to 6 pounds, with short, glossy coats.

Top: *Satin—Red variety*. Bottom: *Silver Marten*.

Tan

As you can see, there are great differences among rabbit breeds, as well as in the varieties within the breeds. Today, many breeders are using selective breeding techniques to try to produce new breeds, so there will always be different kinds of rabbits coming along in the future. It is said that there is no "best" breed of rabbit, because each one has certain advantages, so the "best" one for you is the kind that meets your particular needs and appeals to you the most.

When you buy a purebred rabbit, you should receive its pedigree—a written record that describes the animal's family, going back three generations. You can also buy a crossbreed, which is a rabbit whose parents are of different breeds. Crossbreeds can make good pets, but they cannot be entered in regular rabbit shows.

It is lots of fun to enter a rabbit in a show. Watching your rabbit being judged is exciting and interesting, and you hope that your pet behaves itself and doesn't bite the judge, which occasionally happens. Rabbit shows are held all over the country, and anyone may enter. Here, rabbits within each breed compete with

Show rabbits must meet weight standards.

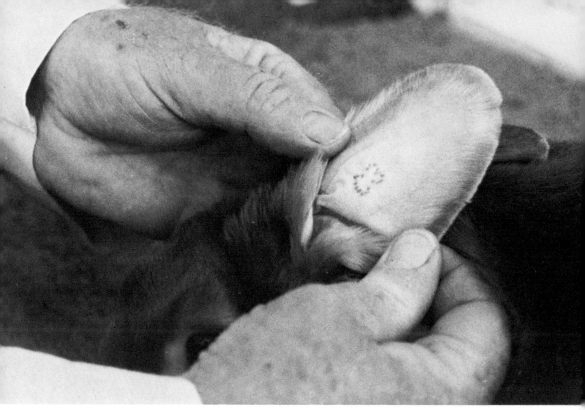

Top: *Judge checks ear tattoo. Every show rabbit must have its own identify-ing ear tattoo.* Bottom: *Judge checks for overall appearance and balance . . .*

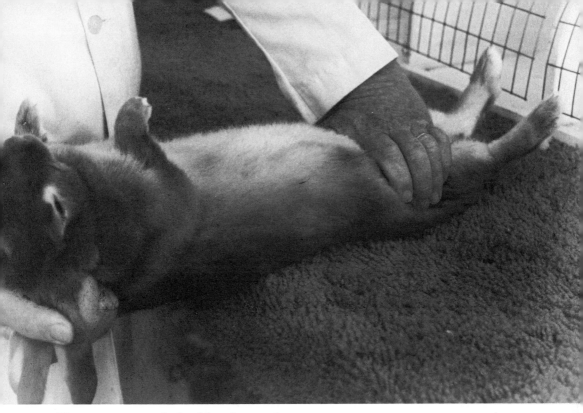

Top: ... *examines the hind legs for straightness* ...
Bottom: ... *examines the front legs* ...

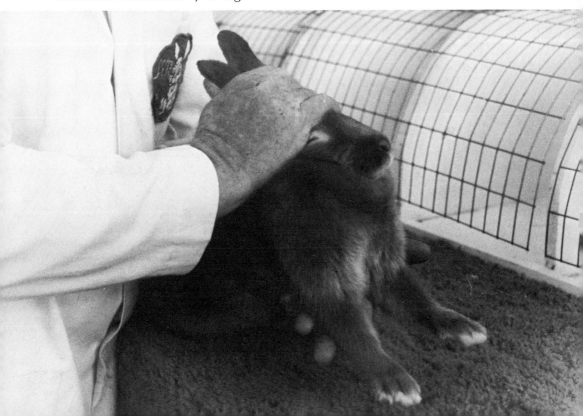

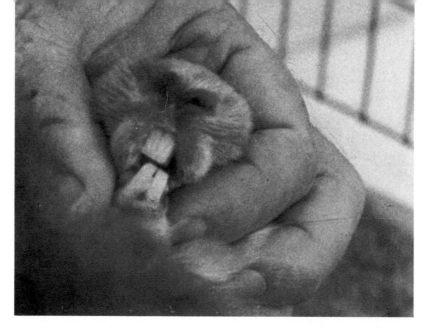

. . . checks the teeth.

each other, and those winning the most points are awarded prizes such as trophies, ribbons, and money. A professional judge thoroughly examines every animal and gives it up to one hundred points, based on its general appearance, balance, fur quality, markings, head structure, and such specifics as its eyes, teeth, legs, feet, toenails, tail, and so on. This point system also stresses the outstanding features of individual breeds. For example, fur breeds like the Rex or Angora are given extra points for their fine coats, whereas rabbits like the Harlequin, Dutch, or English Spot are allotted more for their special markings.

Information about rabbit shows, rabbitries (where rabbits are raised and sold), and clubs and organizations in your area can be obtained by writing to The American Rabbit Breeders Association, P.O. Box 426, Bloomington, Illinois 61701. It is wise to include a self-addressed, stamped envelope with your request.

Domestic rabbits have lived up to ten years. Some say that wild rabbits and hares could live that long if they were raised in captivity, with a good diet and away from predators.

Next time you see a wild cottontail or a jackrabbit feeding along a road or zigzagging across a field, think of the tame rabbit, safe in its cage. Which is the more fortunate? You decide.

Your rabbits can win trophies at shows.

Index